Psalm XXIII

The Lord is my shepherd; I shall not want. ²He maketh me to lie down in green pastures: he leadeth me beside the still waters. ³He restoreth my soul: he leadeth me in the paths of righteousness for his name's sake. ⁴Yea, though I walk through the valley of the shadow of death, I will fear no evil: for thou art with me; thy rod and thy staff they comfort me. ⁵Thou preparest a table before me in the presence of mine enemies: thou anointest my head with oil; my cup runneth over. ⁶Surely goodness and mercy shall follow me all the days of my life: and I will dwell in the house of the Lord for ever.

"Beside the Still Waters." — p. 9.

The Song of Our Syrian Guest

by William Allen Knight

Illustrations and Decorative Designs by Charles Copeland

The Pilgrim Press
Boston · New York · Chicago

———

Set up and electrotyped February, 1904
The Fort Hill Press
Samuel Usher
Boston

To the hand that held the tea-ball & and the faces of the two little maids

Salutation

Three months have gone by since this little child of my heart went out into the world, a strayling in the scanty dress of a booklet. In that time many thousands have looked kindly on the little wanderer and welcomed it into their homes. Letters from everywhere have come in, saying in effect: "It came to my door yesterday, and its voice has been sweet to me, and I am glad to have it stay with me." For all this I am most thankful. But it is hard to realize that the small circle of those who loved this story a few months ago has grown now to a multitude.

Surely none of us ought to be surprised that our story has itself grown under all this kindness, after the manner of children. Indeed, as we are sending it forth newly clothed, I find that it is larger by half than when I last prepared it for journeying.

I am set to wondering whether it will not grow quite away from me and have a life of its own. Healthy children do that very thing usually, and wise parents are willing to have it so.

But I cannot cease to remember that this story is out of my own life. It lay in my heart unborn for long. It came forth in a time of shock and pain. There is One who knows why its face is unmarred and bright with the gladness of trust. I think God has let it speak to so many hearts for this reason.

Go then, little story; be bearer of thy message of cheer and glad restfulness. I cannot follow thee into lives that need to hear thy voice; but speak thou to them, and I shall be content.

Yet I know, friends of mine, that as you look up somewhere in the world from these pages, you will want to ask me a question.

It has been asked and answered many times already. Because I know some of you are in sick-rooms, some are lonely and some companioned by grief, some are poor and some for the time are misunderstood, some are discouraged and some feel themselves little loved, some are young and cannot find their way, and some are old and wayworn, — because I know all of you have need of the Shepherd's watch, I want to answer your question. Yes, we did indeed have such a guest, a man whose home was among the Syrian shepherds, a man who well knew the life which rightly interprets the Shepherd Psalm.

I give my word that this story's message about the Psalm's meaning is straight from David's land. We had such a guest and he told us these things out of the life of his people, as we sat together one night over fragrant cups of tea.

W. A. K.

Boston, January, 1904.

Can there be anything more poetic than this life of the Syrian shepherd? It ought to be religious, too. Far, far away, out on the lone mountain, with the everlasting hills around, and heaven above, pure, blue, and high, and still. There go and worship in solemn silence and soul-subduing solitude, worship the Most High God in his temple not made with hands.

And now the lights are out in the village, the shepherds are asleep by the side of their flocks, the tinkling bell from the fold falls faintly on the still night air, and the watch-dog bays drowsily from his kennel at the gate. Good night, fair world; 'tis time to seek repose. Let us first read and meditate upon that delightful chapter, the tenth of St. John, where our blessed Saviour appropriates all these characters of a good shepherd to himself.

"The Land and the Book."

The Song of Our Syrian Guest

"Faduel Moghabghab," said our guest, laughing as he leaned over the tea-table toward two little maids, vainly trying to beguile their willing and sweetly puckered lips into pronouncing his name. "Faduel Moghabghab," he repeated in syllables, pointing to the card he had passed to them. "Accent the u and drop those g's which your little throats cannot manage," he went on kindly,

**he Song of Our Syrian Guest** while the merriment sparkled in his lustrous dark eyes, and his milk-white teeth, seen through his black moustache as he laughed, added beauty to his delicate and vivacious face.

He was a man of winsome mind, this Syrian guest of ours, and the spirituality of his culture was as marked as the refinement of his manners. We shall long remember him for the tales told that evening of his home in Ainzehalta on the slope of the Syrian mountains, but longest of all for what he said out of the memories of his youth about a shepherd song.

" It was out of the shepherd life of my country," he remarked, " that there came long ago that sweetest religious song ever written — the Twenty-third Psalm."

After the ripple of his merriment with the children had passed he turned to me with a face now serious and pensive, and said: " Ah, so many things familiar to us are strange to you of America."

" Yes," I answered, " and no doubt because of this we often make mistakes which are more serious than mispronunciation of your modern names."

He smiled pleasantly, then with earnestness said: " So many things in the life of my people, the same now as in the days of old, have been woven into the words of the Bible and into the conceptions of religious ideas as expressed there; you of the Western world, not knowing these things as they are, often misunderstand what is written, or at least fail to get a correct impression from it."

" Tell us about some of these," I ventured, with a parental glance at two listening little faces.

The Song of Our Syrian Guest

After mentioning several instances, he went on: " And there is the shepherd psalm: I find that it is taken among you as having two parts, the first under the figure of shepherd life, the second turning to the figure of a banquet with the host and the guest."

" Oh, we have talked about that," said my lady of the teacups as she dangled the tea-ball with a connoisseur's fondness, " and we have even said that we wished the wonderful little psalm could have been finished in the one figure of shepherd life."

" It seems to us," I added, wishing to give suitable support to my lady's rather brave declaration of our sense of a literary flaw in the matchless psalm, " it seems to us to lose the sweet, simple melody and to close with strange, heavy chords when it changes to a scene of banquet hospitality. Do you mean that it actually keeps the shepherd figure to the end?"

"Certainly, good friends."

With keen personal interest I asked him to tell us how we might see it as a shepherd psalm throughout. So we listened and he talked, over the cooling teacups.

"It is all, all a simple shepherd psalm," he began. "See how it runs through the round of shepherd life from first word to last."

With softly modulated voice that had the rhythm of music and the hush of veneration in it, he quoted: "'The Lord is my shepherd; I shall not want.'

"There is the opening strain of its music; in that chord is sounded the key-note which is never lost till the plaintive melody dies away at the song's end. All that follows is that thought put in varying light."

The Song of Our Syrian Guest I wish it were possible to reproduce here the light in his face and the interchange of tones in his mellow voice as he went on. He talked of how the varied needs of the sheep and the many-sided care of the shepherd are pictured with masterly touch in the short sentences of the psalm.

"Each is distinct and adds something too precious to be merged and lost," he said.

"'He maketh me to lie down in green pastures,' — nourishment, rest. 'He leadeth me beside the still waters,' — the scene changes and so does the meaning. You think here of quietly flowing streams; so you get one more picture of rest; but you miss one of the finest scenes in shepherd life and one of the rarest blessings of the soul that is led of God. All through the day's roaming the shepherd keeps one

thing in mind.　He must lead his
flock to a drinking-place.　The refreshment of good water makes the
coveted hour of all the day; the spot
where it is found amid the rough, water-
less hills and plains is the crowning token
of the shepherd's unfailing thoughtfulness.
When at last the sheep are led 'beside
the still waters,' how good it is, after the
dust and heat of the sheep-walks!

"Would you get the shepherd meaning
here?　Then remember that streams are
few in the shepherd country of Bible lands.
The shepherds do not rely on them.　Even
where streams are found, their beds and
banks are usually broken and their flow
rough.　Sheep are timid and fear a current of water, as they well may,
for they are easily
carried down stream
because of their
wool."

 " Poor things, how do they ever get a good drink? " exclaimed one of the two little maids, whose heart was always open lovingly to animals.

" The shepherd sees to that, doesn't he ? " said the other timidly, with earnest eyes set on our guest.

His face beamed with winsome relish of these tributes to his success. " Yes, the sheep would indeed have a hard time finding water to drink, were it not that the shepherd sees to that."

The playfulness faded from his eyes and the shadow of manhood's years was there as he said to me: " Brother, you and I have learned how much is in that question and answer. How would we get the refreshment we need in the rough world, if the Shepherd did not see to that ? But he does, he does! "

His face brightened again as he  turned to the four blue eyes across the table.

" Shall I tell you how the shepherd sees to it that the sheep have a good drink every day? Listen:

" There are wells and fountains all through the vast regions where the flocks roam, and in some parts there are cisterns, though the sheep like the living water best. The shepherds know where these drinking-places are all through the treeless country where streams are few. It is a fine sight to see the shepherds bring their flocks 'beside the still waters' at some well or fountain, while the wide, silent country over which they and many other sheep have wandered, spreads all around them, and the full expanse of the sky arches over them.

" The shepherd makes a certain sound:

all his sheep lie down and are quiet. Then he fills the drinking-troughs. The bubbling of the fountain, or the current, if it be by a stream, is no longer there to trouble the sheep. They can drink now undisturbed. This is the delicate meaning of that word 'still.' As the Hebrew words put it, 'He leadeth beside the waters of quietness.'

"Then the waiting sheep hear a whistle or a call. They never misunderstand; they know their shepherd's voice and never respond to the wrong shepherd if several flocks have come up together. And strangest of all, the sheep come up by groups; the shepherd makes them understand. So in groups he leads them until they stand 'beside the still waters.' And, oh, how they drink, with the shepherd standing near!"

After a pause, with a far-off look in his

eyes, he said, "It is a beautiful scene, so beautiful that St. John has used it in picturing heaven." A smile broke

over his face as he quoted: "'The Lamb that is in the midst of the throne shall be their shepherd, and shall guide them unto fountains of waters of life.'"

No one spoke as he sat turning his tea-cup. A tear started from his dropped eyes. Presently he seemed to recall himself.

"But I must tell you one more scene that comes to my memory whenever I read the words, '**He leadeth me beside the still waters.**' It would make a beautiful picture if some one would paint it.

"Up in the mountainsides of Lebanon, where my kinsmen have long been shep-herds, often there are no regular drinking-places, such as the wells and fountains on the plains. But as the shepherd leads his sheep over the rough slopes he finds many

The Song of Our Syrian Guest a spring and sees its rivulet noisily running down a crevice. His sheep need water. They cannot drink from the leaping little stream. What does he do? He finds a suitable turn or nook in its course; he walls it up with a little dam and so holds the water till it forms a quiet pool. Then, right there on the open hills, he leads his sheep 'beside the still waters.' I know of nothing more fit to picture the Shepherd's care of souls that trust him than that scene up there on the mountainside."

While our thoughts were carried away to these scenes of thirsty flocks drinking, I chanced to notice that the tea-ball was again quietly at work. As we sat thinking on that picture up in the mountain, a good hand offered our guest a fresh cup. He received it with a low bow, sipped it in quiet, then with a grateful smile began speaking again:

" 'He restoreth my soul.' You know," he said, turning to me, " that soul means the life or one's self in the Hebrew writings."

Then addressing us all he went on: " There are perilous places for the sheep on all sides, and they seem never to learn to avoid them. The shepherd must ever be on the watch. And there are private fields and sometimes gardens and vineyards here and there in the shepherd country; if the sheep stray into them and be caught there it is forfeited to the owner of the land. So, 'He restoreth my soul' means, ' The shepherd brings me back and rescues me from fatal and forbidden places.' "

" ' Restores me when wandering,' is the way it is put in one of our hymns," I interposed.

"Ah, sir, that is it exactly," he answered, "'Restores me when wandering!'

"'He leadeth me in the paths of righteousness for his name's sake.' Often have I roamed through the shepherd country in my youth and seen how hard it is to choose the right path for the sheep; one leads to a precipice, another to a place where the sheep cannot find the way back; and the shepherd was always going ahead, 'leading' them in the right paths, proud of his good name as a shepherd.

"Some paths that are right paths still lead through places that have deadly perils. 'Yea, though I walk through the valley of the shadow of death,' is the way the psalm touches this fact in shepherd life. This way of naming the valley is very true to our country. I remember one near my home called 'the valley of robbers,'

"The Valley of the Shadow of Death."

and another, 'the ravine of the raven.' You see 'the valley of the shadow of death' is a name drawn from my country's old custom.

" 'For thou art with me.' Ah, how could more be put into few words! With the sheep, it matters not what the surroundings are, nor how great the perils and hardships; if only the shepherd is with them, they are content. There is no finer picture of the way of peace for the troubled in all the world.

" To show how much the presence of the shepherd counts for the welfare of the sheep I can think of nothing better than the strange thing I now tell you. It is quite beyond the usual, daily care on which the flock depends so fondly. But I have seen it more than once.

" Sometimes, in spite of all the care of the shepherd and his dogs, a wolf will get

The Song of Our Syrian Guest into the very midst of the flock. The sheep are wild with fright. They run and leap and make it impossible to get at the foe in their midst, who at that very moment may be fastening his teeth in the throat of a helpless member of the flock. But the shepherd is with them. He knows what to do even at such a time. He leaps to a rock or hillock that he may be seen and heard. Then he lifts his voice in a long call, something like a wolf's cry: 'Ooh! ooh!'

"On hearing this, the sheep remember the shepherd; they heed his voice; and, strange to tell, the poor, timid creatures, which were helpless with terror before, instantly rush with all their strength into a solid mass. The pressure is irresistible; the wolf is overcome; frequently he is crushed to death, while the shepherd stands there on a rock crying, 'Ooh! ooh!' 'I will fear no evil: for thou art with me.'"

He paused, looking questioningly at one and another.

" Yes," I said at last, " 'in all these things we are more than conquerors through him that loved us.'" He bowed his satisfaction in silence.

" 'Thy rod and thy staff' — this also is true to life; the double expression covers the whole round of protecting care. For the shepherds carry a crook for guiding the sheep and a weapon suitable for defending them, the rod and the staff; one for aiding them in places of need along peaceful ways, the other for defense in perils of robbers and wild beasts. This saying describes with the ease of mastery how much those words mean, 'Thou art with me.'

The Song of Our Syrian Guest

" And what shall I say of the next words, 'Thy rod and thy staff they comfort me'? Ah, madam, you should see the sheep cuddle near the shepherd to understand that word, 'They comfort me.' The shepherd's call 'Ta-a-a-a, ho-o-o,' and the answering patter of feet as the sheep hurry to him, are fit sounds to be chosen out of the noisy world to show what comfort God gives to souls that heed his voice; and those sounds have been heard in my country this day as they were the day this shepherd psalm was written!"

He sat in silence a moment musing as if the sound were in his ear.

With quiet animation he lifted his thin hand and continued: "Now here is where you drop the shepherd figure and put in a banquet and so lose

the fine climax of completeness in the shepherd's care."

It need not be said that we were eager listeners now, for our guest was all aglow with memories of his far-off homeland and we felt that we were about to see new rays of light flash from this rarest gem in the song-treasury of the world.

" 'Thou preparest a table before me in the presence of mine enemies.' " In the same hushed voice in which he quoted these words he added: " Ah, to think that the shepherd's highest skill and heroism should be lost from view as the psalm begins to sing of it, and only an indoor banquet thought of!" Again he sat a little time in quiet. Then he said:

"The word for table here means simply 'something spread out' and so a prepared meal, however it is set forth. There is no higher task of the shepherd

 in my country than to go from time to time to study places and examine the grass and find a good and safe feeding-place for his sheep. All his skill and often great heroism are called for. There are many poisonous plants in the grass and the shepherd must find and avoid them. The sheep will not eat certain poisonous things, but there are some which they will eat, one kind of poisonous grass in particular. A cousin of mine once lost three hundred sheep by a mistake in this hard task.

"Then there are snake holes in some kinds of ground, and, if they be not driven away, the snakes bite the noses of the sheep. The shepherd sometimes burns the fat of hogs along the ground to do this. Sometimes the shepherd finds ground where moles have worked their holes just under the surface. Snakes lie in these holes with their heads sticking up  ready to bite the grazing sheep. The shepherds know how to drive them away as they go along ahead of the sheep.

" And around the feeding-ground which the shepherd thus prepares, in holes and caves in the hillsides there are jackals, wolves, hyenas, and panthers, too, and the bravery and skill of the shepherd are at the highest point in closing up these dens with stones or slaying the wild beasts with his long-bladed knife. Of nothing do you hear shepherds boasting more proudly than of their achievements in this part of their care of flocks.

" And now," he exclaimed with a beaming countenance and suppressed feeling, as if pleading for recognition of the lone shepherd's bravest act of devotion to his sheep, " and now do you not see the

shepherd figure in that quaint line, 'Thou preparest a table before me in the presence of mine enemies' ? "

" Yes," I answered; " and I see that God's care of a man out in the world is a grander thought than that of seating him at an indoor banquet-table."

" But what about anointing the head with oil and the cup running over? Go on, my friend."

" Oh, there begins the beautiful picture at the end of the day. The psalm has sung of the whole round of the day's wandering, all the needs of the sheep, all the care of the shepherd. Now the psalm closes with the last scene of the day. At the door of the sheepfold the shepherd stands and ' the rodding of the sheep ' takes place. The shepherd stands, turning his body to let the sheep pass; he is the door, as Christ said of himself. With

"The Rodding of the Sheep."

his rod he holds back the sheep while  he inspects them one by one as they pass into the fold. He has the horn filled with olive-oil and he has cedar-tar, and he anoints a knee bruised on the rocks or a side scratched by thorns. And here comes one that is not bruised but is simply worn and exhausted; he bathes its face and head with the refreshing olive-oil and he takes the large two-handled cup and dips it brimming full from the vessel of water provided for that purpose, and he lets the weary sheep drink.

" There is nothing finer in the psalm than this. God's care is not for the wounded only, but for the worn and weary also. 'Thou anointest my head with oil; my cup runneth over.'

" And then, when the day is done and the sheep are snug within the fold, what contentment, what rest under the starry

The Song of Our Syrian Guest

sky! Then comes the thought of deepest repose and comfort: '**Surely goodness and mercy shall follow me all the days of my life**,' as they have through all the wanderings of the day now ended.

"The song dies away as the heart that God has watched and tended breathes this grateful vow before the roaming of the day is forgotten in sleep: '**I will**' — not shall, but will; for it is a decision, a settled purpose, a holy vow — '**I will dwell in the house of the Lord for ever**.' And the song ends, and the sheep are at rest, safe in the good shepherd's fold."

Do you wonder that ever since that night we have called this psalm The Song of Our Syrian Guest?

Sidelights

Shepherd Life in Bible Lands

PROFESSOR GEORGE E. POST

The American College, Beyrout, Syria

" The same regions which furnished the vast flocks in ancient times are still noted for their sheep. All the plateaus east of the Jordan and the mountains of Palestine and Syria are pasture-grounds for innumerable flocks and herds. They require water but once a day, and, where they cannot get it from perennial streams, they find it in the innumerable wells, fountains and cisterns. The descendants of the same shepherds who tended flocks in Bible days still occupy the great sheep-walks of Palestine.

The Song of Our Syrian Guest

"The care of sheep is the subject of frequent allusion in Scripture. The shepherd leads (not drives) them to pasture and water (Ps. 23; 77:20; 78:52; 80:1); protects them at the risk of his life (John 10:15). To keep them from the cold and rain and beasts, he collects them in caves (1 Sam. 24:3) or enclosures built of rough stones (Num. 32:16; Judg. 5:16; Zeph. 2:6; John 10:1). The sheep know their shepherd, and heed his voice (John 10:4). It is one of the most interesting spectacles to see a number of flocks of thirsty sheep brought by their several shepherds to be watered at a fountain. Each flock, in obedience to the call of its own shepherd, lies down, awaiting its turn. The shepherd of one flock calls his sheep in squads, draws water for them, pours it into the troughs, and, when the squad has done, orders it away by sounds which the sheep perfectly understand, and calls up another squad. When the whole of one flock is watered, its shepherd signals to it, and the sheep rise and move leisurely away, while another flock comes in a similar manner to the troughs, and so on, until all the flocks are watered. The sheep never make any mistake as to who whistles to them or calls to them. 'They know not the voice of strangers' (John 10: 5). Sometimes they are called by names (John 10: 3). Syrian sheep are usually white (Ps. 147: 16; Isa. 1: 18; Dan. 7: 9), but some are brown (Gen. 30: 32–42; Revised Version 'black'). No animal mentioned in Scripture compares in symbolical interest and importance with the sheep. It is alluded to about five hundred times."

The Singing Pilgrim

A CHARACTERIZATION OF THE TWENTY-THIRD PSALM

HENRY WARD BEECHER

"The Twenty-third Psalm is the night-ingale of the psalms. It is small, of a homely feather, singing shyly out of obscurity; but, oh, it has filled the air of the whole world with melodious joy, greater than the heart can conceive! Blessed be the day on which that psalm was born!

"What would you say of a pilgrim commissioned of God to travel up and down the earth singing a strange melody, which, when once heard, caused him to forget whatever sorrow he had? And so the singing angel goes on his way through all  lands, singing in the language of every nation, driving away trouble by the pulses of the air which his tongue moves with divine power. Behold just such an one! This pilgrim God has sent to speak in every language on the globe. It has charmed more griefs to rest than all the philosophy of the world. It has remanded to their dungeon more felon thoughts, more black doubts, more thieving sorrows, than there are sands on the seashore. It has comforted the noble host of the poor. It has sung courage to the army of the disappointed. It has poured balm and consolation into the heart of the sick, of captives in dungeons, of widows in their pinching griefs, of orphans in their loneliness. Dying soldiers have died easier as it was read to them; ghastly hospitals have been illuminated;

 The Song of Our Syrian Guest it has visited the prisoner and broken his chains, and, like Peter's angel, led him forth in imagination, and sung him back to his home again. It has made the dying Christian slave freer than his master, and consoled those whom, dying, he left behind, mourning not so much that he was gone as because they were left behind and could not go too.

"Nor is its work done. It will go on singing to your children and my children, and to their children, through all the generations of time; nor will it fold its wings till the last pilgrim is safe, and time ended; and then it shall fly back to the bosom of God, whence it issued, and sound on, mingled with all those sounds of celestial joy which make heaven musical forever."